Historical Data Collection of Suzhou Industrial and Commercial Archives

苏 州 市 工 商 业 档 案 史 料 丛 编

Bu Jianmin Editor-in-Chief

卜鉴民　主编

近现代中国苏州丝绸档案

The Archives of Suzhou Silk in Modern and Contemporary Times

Soochow University Press

图书在版编目(CIP)数据

近现代中国苏州丝绸档案 / 卜鉴民主编. —苏州：苏州大学出版社,2017.9
ISBN 978-7-5672-2242-7

Ⅰ.①近… Ⅱ.①卜… Ⅲ.①丝绸工业－经济史－苏州－近现代 Ⅳ.①F426.81

中国版本图书馆CIP数据核字(2017)第237455号

近现代中国苏州丝绸档案

卜鉴民　主编

责任编辑　王　亮

苏州大学出版社出版发行
(地址：苏州市十梓街1号　邮编：215006)
苏州市深广印刷有限公司印装
(地址：苏州市高新区浒关工业园青花路6号2号厂房　邮编：215151)

开本 889 mm×1 194 mm　1/16　印张 4.75　字数 61千
2017年9月第1版　2017年9月第1次印刷
ISBN 978-7-5672-2242-7　　定价：68.00元

苏州大学版图书若有印装错误,本社负责调换
苏州大学出版社营销部　电话：0512 - 65225020
苏州大学出版社网址　http://www.sudapress.com

编 委 会

主　任　钱　斌

副主任　沈慧瑛　卜鉴民　虞爱国

委　员　甘　戈　吴　芳　彭聚营　朱亚鹏

　　　　陈　鑫　王雯昕　许　瑶　张旭东

　　　　周玲凤　陈明怡　李艳兰　赵　颖

　　　　谢震香　董文弢　盛　明　栾清照

主　编　卜鉴民

副主编　甘　戈　吴　芳　陈　鑫　杨　韫

编　辑　周　济　栾清照　张　婧　苏　锦

　　　　周小琳

摄　影　王颖华

前言 Preface

丝绸,是中国所独有的"东方式智慧",是中西方文明沟通的重要媒介,更是全世界共同的文化财富。

然而,由于丝织品本身对温湿度等保存环境有着近乎苛刻的要求,在一代又一代的传承中,它们逐渐失去了应有的柔软与光泽。并且,随着社会的转型,手工作坊、传统丝织企业陆续关闭,丝织技艺也逐渐失传。

近现代中国苏州丝绸档案,是 19 世纪到 20 世纪末期,苏州丝绸产业在技术研发、生产管理、营销贸易、对外交流过程中直接形成的,由纸质文图和丝绸样本实物组成的,具有保存价值的原始记录,共计 29592 卷。这批丝绸档案因其罕有、全面而成为苏州市工商档案管理中心(以下简称"中心")的"镇馆之宝"。

透过一卷卷丝绸档案,我们看到了无与伦比的美,也看到了沉甸甸的责任。中心在接收这批丝绸档案之初,就面临着丝织技艺濒危下的强大压力——保护与传承。无论是工艺单、意匠图还是丝绸样本,这些丝绸档案倘若不去保护,失了传承,便意味着破坏。

幸运的是,中心采取的一系列措施,都行之有效。2015年,经国务院办公厅批准,中心加挂"苏州中国丝绸档案馆"牌子,这一国内首家和唯一一家专门的丝绸档案馆落户苏州。在我们的呼吁下,越来越多的专家、学者开始重视这批档案,研究丝绸档案的论文和书籍在不断增多。以我们的星星之火,点燃了国人对丝绸档案研究的热情。近现代中国苏州丝绸档案,这是有着国际性价值的文献资料,它应当被世界所熟知。

As the unique Chinese "oriental wisdom", silk is the important carrier of the communication between Eastern and Western cultures and the common cultural wealth of the whole world.

However, due to their harsh environment requirements to preserve like temperature and humidity, silk productions have gradually lost the original softness and lustre from generation to generation. What's more, silk weaving technology has gradually died out with the social transformation and the closure of manual workshops and traditional silk weaving factories.

The archives of Suzhou silk in modern and contemporary times are directly formed during the process of technical research, production management, trading and marketing, and foreign exchanges of Suzhou silk enterprises and organizations from the 19th century to the end of the 20th century. These archives containing 29,592 volumes are composed of different forms including written records and silk samples with high preservation value. The silk archives are preserved in Suzhou Industrial and Commercial Archives Administration (hereafter referred as the administration) as "the most valuable treasure" for the rareness and completeness.

The silk archives not only show the incomparable beauty of silk but also place heavy responsibilities on the administration. The moment the administration received these archives, intense pressure has been put on it to protect and inherit the silk technology on the verge of extinction. No protection equals destruction. If the silk archives including technical sheets, pattern grids and silk samples were not under protection, there would be no silk treasure to be inherited.

Fortunately, the administration has carried out a series of measures that work well. With the approval of the General Office of the State Council in 2015, the administration added a brand named "Suzhou China Silk Archives", which meant the first and the only professional silk archives had settled in Suzhou. Following the appeal by the administration, more and more experts and scholars begin to pay attention to the silk archives along with the increasing theses and books on the research of silk archives. The administration's efforts are like a single spark that lights the public's enthusiasm for the research of silk archives. The archives of Suzhou silk in modern and contemporary times, as documentary data with international value, is worth knowing by the world.

历史缩影
Historical Miniature

一、19世纪—20世纪初期的丝绸档案 / 3
Silk Archives Ranging from the 19th Century to the Early 20th Century

二、20世纪初期—20世纪中期的丝绸档案 / 6
Silk Archives Ranging from the Beginning to the Middle of the 20th Century

三、20世纪中期—20世纪末期的丝绸档案 / 9
Silk Archives Ranging from the Middle to the End of the 20th Century

目录
Contents

一、丝绸贸易档案 / 23
Silk Trading Archives

二、丝绸商标档案 / 31
Silk Trademark Archives

三、科技档案 / 35
Science and Technology Archives

匠心传承
Craft Art Inheritance

3 古韵今声
Classical Styles in Modern Life

一、人类非物质文化遗产——苏州缂丝 / 45
Intangible Cultural Heritage of Humanity—Suzhou K'o-ssy

二、人类非物质文化遗产——苏州宋锦 / 47
Intangible Cultural Heritage of Humanity—Suzhou Song Brocade

三、国家级非物质文化遗产——苏绣 / 49
National Intangible Cultural Heritage—Suzhou Embroidery

四、省级非物质文化遗产——漳缎 / 51
Provincial Intangible Cultural Heritage—Zhangduan

五、省级非物质文化遗产——四经绞罗 / 53
Provincial Intangible Cultural Heritage—Four-and-complex Gauze

六、省级非物质文化遗产——纱罗 / 54
Provincial Intangible Cultural Heritage—Gauze

4 惊艳世界
Striving Surprise to the World

一、塔夫绸 / 57
Taffeta

二、真丝印花绸 / 59
Printing Silk

三、APEC 服装面料 / 61
APEC Fabric

5 锦绣风采
Fantastic Demeanor

绫、绸、缎、葛、绉、纺、罗 / 65
Ghatpot, Silk fabric, Satin, Grosgrain, Crepe, Habotai, Leno

绢、锦、绒、绡、绨、呢、纱 / 66
Spun silk, Brocade, Velvet, Chiffon, Bengaline, Suiting silk, Gauze

農商總長　田文烈

右給振亞織物無限公司

中華民國六年七月　日

所在地　江蘇蘇州倉街設江蘇上海後馬路乾記弄三號分公司

姓名住址

本總銀數四萬元

業織物

號振亞織物無限公司

照一體保護合將該公司聲明各欵列後

請設立註冊到部核與條例相符應

照章無限公司遵照公司條例第

历史缩影
Historical Miniature

一、19世纪—20世纪初期的丝绸档案
Silk Archives Ranging from the 19th Century to the Early 20th Century

1908年苏州丝绸企业与官方的来往文书
Intercourse document between Suzhou silk factories and officials in 1908

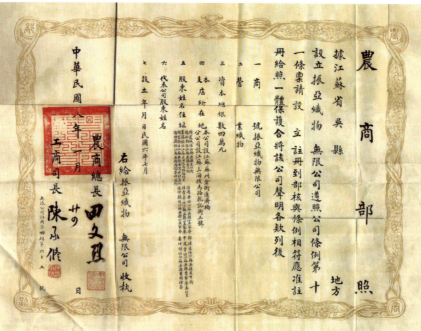

1919年农商部照
Picture of the Ministry of Agriculture and Commerce in 1919

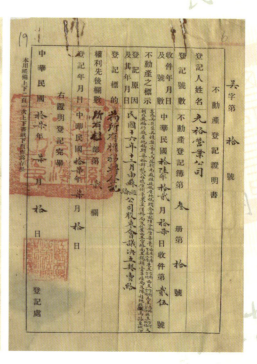

1928年苏州丝绸企业不动产登记证明书
Certificate of real estate registration of Suzhou silk factories in 1928

1929年西湖博览会陈列品清单
List of exhibit at the West Lake Exposition in 1929

文官补子
Square badge

淡青色云纹花卉实地纱料
Gauze with clouds and flowers on light blueish tabby ground

米色地团窠花卉纹彩库锦
Caiku brocade with rounded flowers on beige ground

柞蚕蜀锦
Tussah Shu brocade

二、20世纪初期—20世纪中期的丝绸档案
Silk Archives Ranging from the Beginning to the Middle of the 20th Century

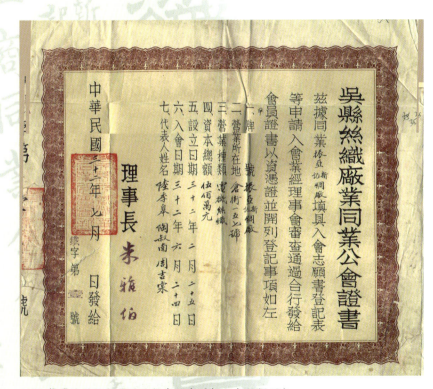

1943年吴县丝织厂业同业公会证书（振亚新记绸厂）
Certificate of Wuxian County Silk Industrial Guild in 1943 (Zhenyaxinji Silk Factory)

1943年吴县铁机丝织业同业公会会员证书（振亚新记绸厂）
Membership Certificate of Wuxian County Machine-woven Silk Industrial Guild in 1943 (Zhenyaxinji Silk Weaving Factory)

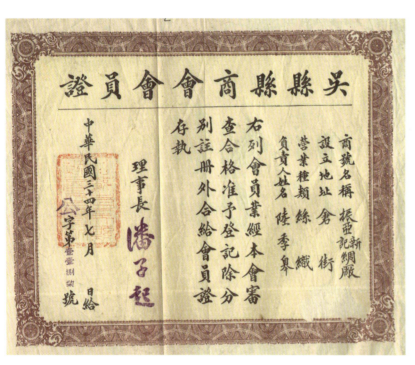

1945年吴县县商会会员证（振亚新记绸厂）
Membership Card of Wuxian County Chamber of Commerce in 1945 (Zhenyaxinji Silk Factory)

1942年丝绸婚书
Silk marriage certificate in 1942

紫色地牡丹纹利库锦
Liku brocade with peonies on violet ground

蓝地花卉织锦缎
Satin brocade with flowers on blue ground

交织宋锦
Jacquard Song brocade

风景古香缎
Satin damask with landscape motif

三、20世纪中期—20世纪末期的丝绸档案
Silk Archives Ranging from the Middle to the End of the 20th Century

1. 像锦织物
Fabrics with portrait or landscape

像锦织物是丝织人像和风景织物的总称，是供装饰和欣赏用的丝织工艺品。中华人民共和国成立后，随着织制像锦画工艺技术的提高，人们怀着对新生活的美好憧憬、期望以及对领袖人物的崇敬，各地有能力的丝织厂纷纷织造以毛泽东主席为主的领袖形象，歌颂伟大领袖毛主席、反映毛主席领袖风采的丝绸画得以大量生产。

Fabrics with portrait or landscape are silk artworks for decorating and appreciating. After the founding of the People's Republic of China, woven brocade painting technology was improved. People had a new vision and expectations of a better life and respect for the leaders. Silk factories weaved the leader images mainly of Chairman Mao one after another. Silk paintings which praised the great leader Chairman Mao and reflected his leadership style were able to be mass-produced.

历史缩影

丝织风景画
Landscape woven by silk

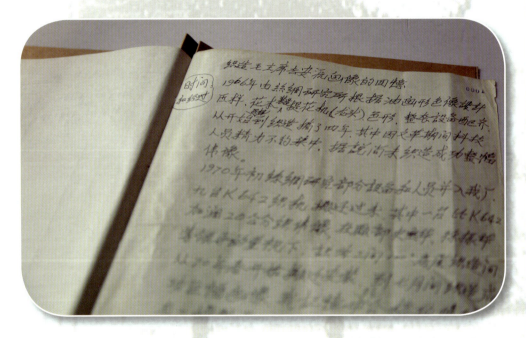
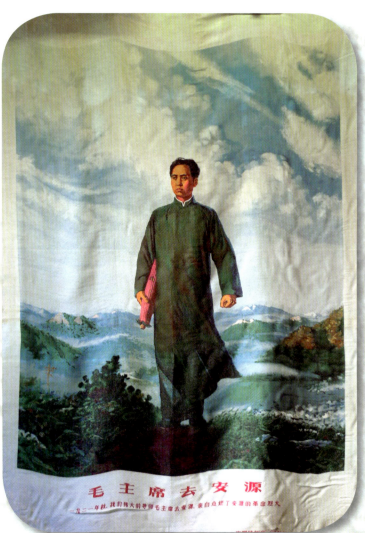

《毛主席去安源》织造回忆录及实物档案
Weaving memoirs and product archives of "Chairman Mao Going to Anyuan"

历史缩影

1960 年像锦织物产品样品说明
Sample description of fabrics with portrait or landscape in 1960

2. 古香缎
Soochow brocade

古香缎是中国传统丝织物，花纹图案以亭台楼阁、花鸟鱼虫或人物故事为主，色彩风格淳朴，主要用于制作女用高级服装和领带、靠垫等装饰用品。此外，部分文学作品也融入设计创作中，如以孙悟空为主题的这一古香缎，精致之外更添妙趣。

Soochow brocade is Chinese traditional silk fabric. The patterns mainly include pavilions, flowers, birds, fish, insects and character stories, in simple color style. It is mainly used for making high-grade female clothing and decoration products like tie, pillow, and so on. Some literature is also absorbed into the creation, like Soochow brocade with Monkey King motif which is both exquisite and interesting.

历史缩影

古香缎 Soochow brocade

近现代中国苏州丝绸档案
The Archives of Suzhou Silk in Modern and Contemporary Times

古香缎
Soochow brocade

古香缎
Soochow brocade

3. 天鹅绒
Velvet

天鹅绒又称漳绒，是中国传统织物之一。由其制成的天鹅绒毯多以人物、花卉、动物、风景等为题材，呈现出国画、油画等多种艺术形式，手法写实，具有独特的艺术风格。

Velvet, also called Zhangrong, is one of Chinese traditional silk productions. Velvet carpets present multiple art forms like Chinese paintings and oil paintings on the themes of characters, flowers, animals and landscape with unique art styles.

K157　六骏　Six coursers
Size: 120 x 180 cm

《六骏图》天鹅绒毯样本、照片及实物档案　Sample, picture and product archives of velvet carpet "Six Coursers"

历史缩影

K136　熊貓　Panda
Size : 120 x 180 cm

《熊猫》天鹅绒毯样本及照片档案
Sample and picture archives of velvet carpet "Panda"

《麦加》天鹅绒毯样本
Sample of velvet carpet "Mecca"

《最后一次晚餐》天鹅绒毯样本
Sample of velvet carpet "The Last Supper"

4. 卡通印花绸
Cartoon printing silk

随着中西方文化交流的增多，中外文化互相影响，丝绸图案中出现了意趣盎然的卡通印花，白雪公主、米老鼠、唐老鸭等卡通形象也为丝绸增添了一抹不一样的色彩。

With the increase of communication between Eastern and Western cultures and the influence on each other, cartoon prints full of interest and charm have been added into the silk patterns, such as Snow White, Mickey Mouse and Donald Duck which make silk more colourful.

一、丝绸贸易档案
Silk Trading Archives

1. 丝绸外销档案
Exported silk archives

该组档案是中华人民共和国成立后出口国外的丝绸产品的档案，展示了中国专为外销设计、生产并输出到世界各地，特别是欧美国家的丝绸织绣品，从中显示出中国丰富灿烂的丝绸文化。大量的订货单档案，记录了苏州丝绸远销全球的历史瞬间，表明丝绸一直是东方文明的重要象征和传播媒介。

These are archives of exported silk productions after the founding of the People's Republic of China. These silk woven and embroidery products from China were specially designed, manufactured and exported to the world, especially to Europe and America. They exhibit the abundant and glorious silk culture of China. The large number of order archives records the historical moment of worldwide export of Suzhou silk products. They indicate that the silk products are always important symbols and media of oriental civilization.

大洋洲
Oceania

澳大利亚
Australia

新西兰
New Zealand

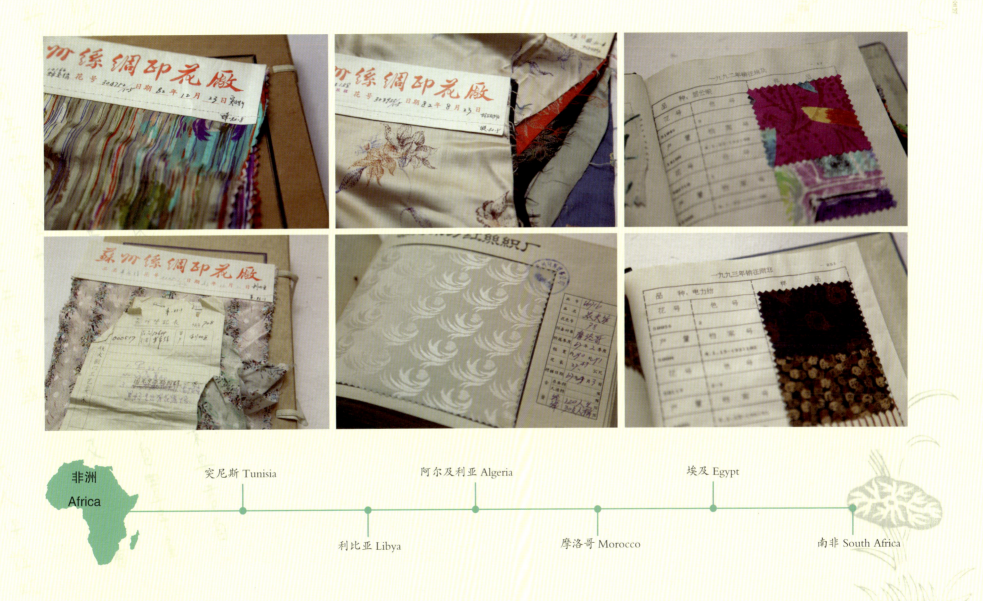

非洲 Africa — 突尼斯 Tunisia — 利比亚 Libya — 阿尔及利亚 Algeria — 摩洛哥 Morocco — 埃及 Egypt — 南非 South Africa

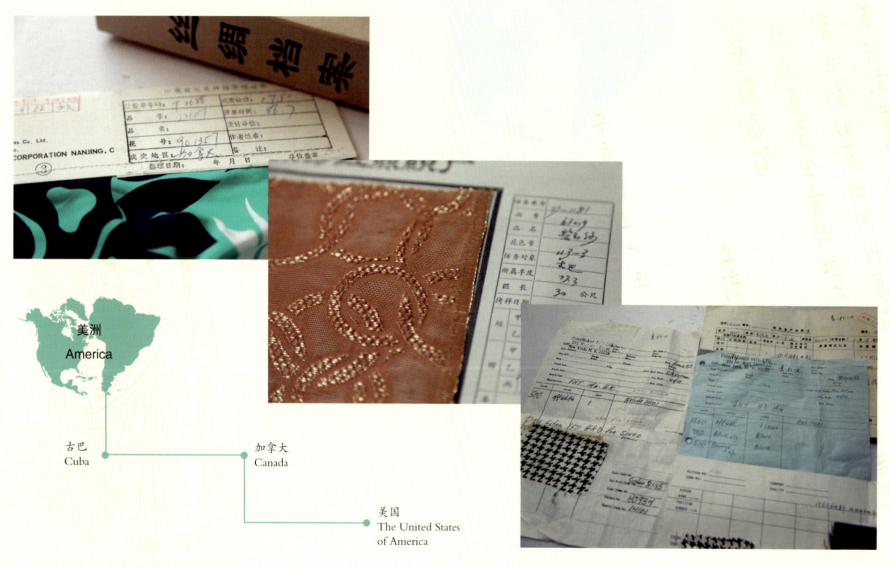

美洲
America

古巴
Cuba

加拿大
Canada

美国
The United States of America

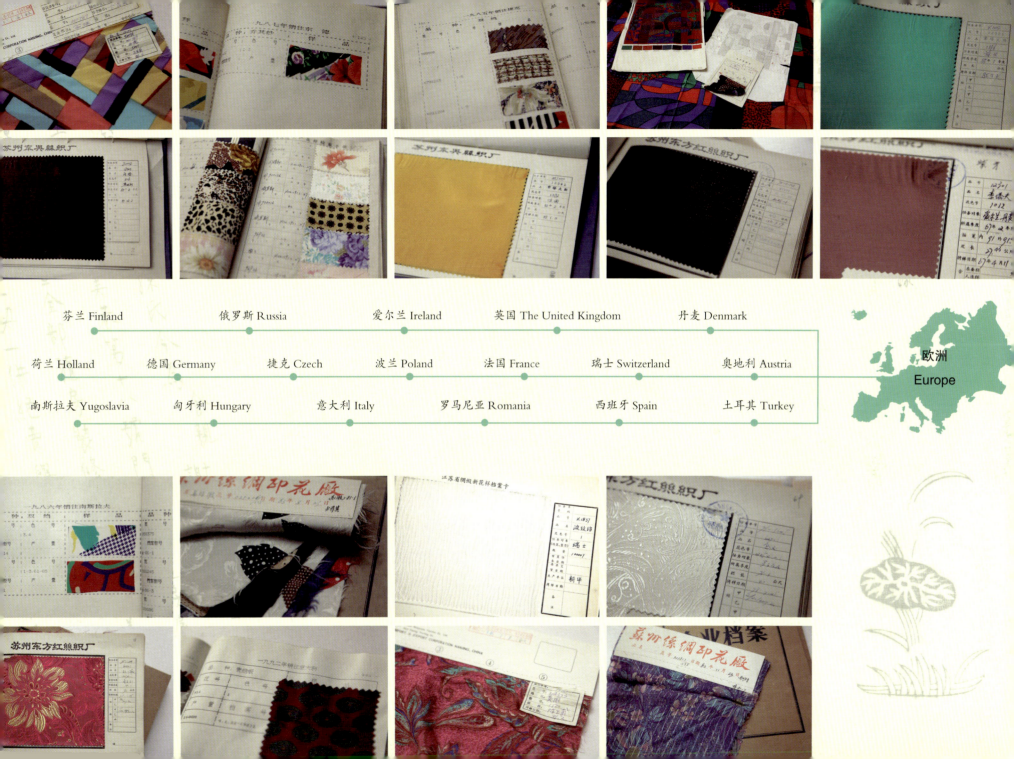

芬兰 Finland	俄罗斯 Russia	爱尔兰 Ireland	英国 The United Kingdom	丹麦 Denmark	
荷兰 Holland	德国 Germany	捷克 Czech	波兰 Poland	法国 France	瑞士 Switzerland	奥地利 Austria
南斯拉夫 Yugoslavia	匈牙利 Hungary	意大利 Italy	罗马尼亚 Romania	西班牙 Spain	土耳其 Turkey

欧洲 Europe

2. 丝绸商贸档案
Silk trading archives

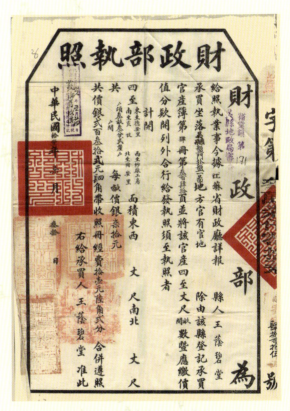

1922年苏纶纺织厂承卖官产的财政部执照
License for Sulun Cotton Mill to sell official property issued by the Ministry of Finance in 1922

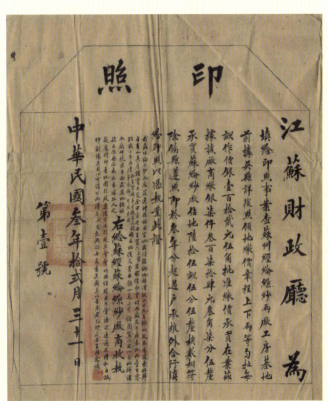

1914年苏纶丝纱两厂工房基地的作价单
Price sheet of the factory bases of Sujing Silk Factory and Sulun Cotton Mill in 1914

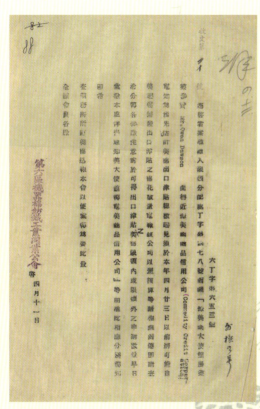

1947年机械纺织同业公会与美国大使馆来往公函
Intercourse official letter between the Machinery-Textile Trade Association and the United States Embassy in 1947

丝绸商贸档案主要包括商业情报、商业机密、生产技术信息等内容，可谓是企业的核心资料。中心馆藏丝绸商贸档案除各丝绸厂家的经营管理制度外，也涵盖了部分客户信息、销售网络等资料，种类较全，内容丰富。

Silk trading archives, as the core element of a company, mainly include business intelligence, trade secret and production technology information. The silk trading archives collected in the administration contain management systems of silk companies as well as partial customers' information and sales network, varied in type and rich in content.

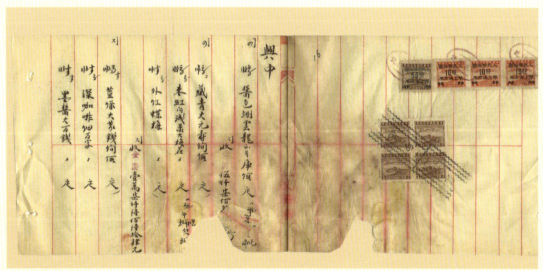

1939年销货客清
Sale list in 1939

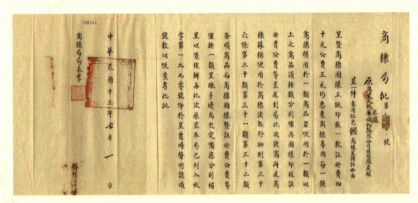

1924年专用红色振亚商标呈请注册书
Application for the registration of the trademark of exclusive red "Zhenya" in 1924

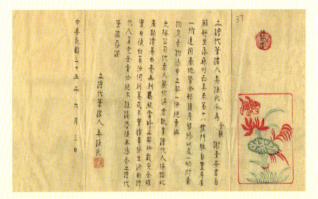

1914年土地契
Land deed in 1914

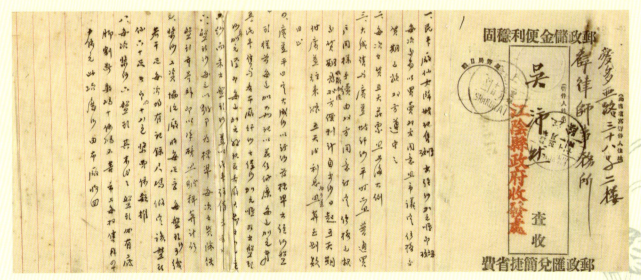

苏纶纱厂销售及进货等情况说明材料
Sales and purchase data of Sulun Cotton Mill

二、丝绸商标档案
Silk Trademark Archives

1932年天官牌商标
The trademark "Tianguan" in 1932

1929年天官牌商标注册证
The trademark registration certificate of brand "Tianguan" in 1929

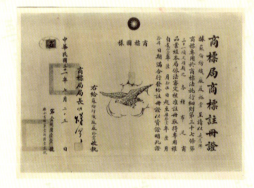

1932年飞鹰牌商标注册证
The trademark registration certificate of brand "Flying Eagle" in 1932

1930年神鹰牌商标注册证
The trademark registration certificate of brand "Mighty Eagle" in 1930

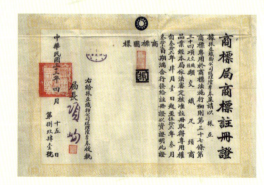

1946年振亚牌商标注册证
The trademark registration certificate of brand "Zhenya" in 1946

匠心传承

丝绸商标档案是丝绸商标注册、管理活动中形成的具有保存利用价值的文件材料。它们是确立和保护注册商标专用权的凭证，是国家档案全宗中具有法律意义的重要的专门档案。

Silk trademark archives are formed during the process of silk trademark registration and management with preservation and use value. As the vouchers to establish and protect the exclusive rights of registered trademarks, they are important specialized archives with legal significance in state archival fonds.

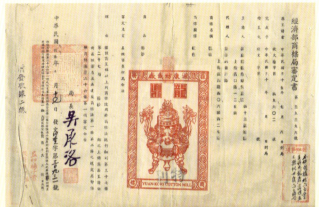 
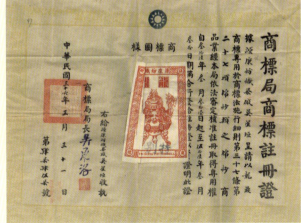 

1946年龙鼎牌商标审定书及商标注册证
The trademark approval and the trademark registration certificate of brand "Dragon Tripod" in 1946

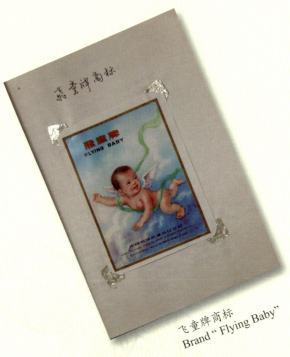

飞童牌商标
Brand "Flying Baby"

水榭牌商标
Brand "Waterhall"

钟山牌和苏城牌商标
Brand "Zhongshan" and "Sucheng"

金桂牌商标
Brand "Jingui"

姑苏牌商标
Brand "Gusu"

灵岩牌商标
Brand "Lingyan"

湖心亭牌商标
Brand "Mid-lake Pavilion"

剑池牌商标
Brand "Sword Pond"

丝路牌商标
Brand "Silu"

三、科技档案
Science and Technology Archives

1. 工艺单
Technical archives

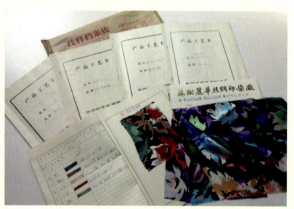
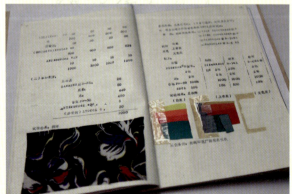

这些档案从技术层面展示出丝绸产品生产的工艺过程。与中国匠人习惯口耳相传以至于技艺变形、人逝技绝不同的是，这些不可再生的原始档案，保存了产品的原料构成、工艺参数、纹样色彩等技术细节。不同历史时段的审美风尚、衣冠体制得到了多样化的存档，同时也为丝绸产品的开发提供了创意。

These archives show the technological process of the silk products. These irreversible original archives preserve the technical details of products such as material compositions, technology parameters and pattern colors. The aesthetic fashions and garment systems in different history periods are also reserved diversely. This is different from the way of "word of mouth" used by traditional Chinese craftsmen, which results in the distortion and even disappearance after craftsmen's death.

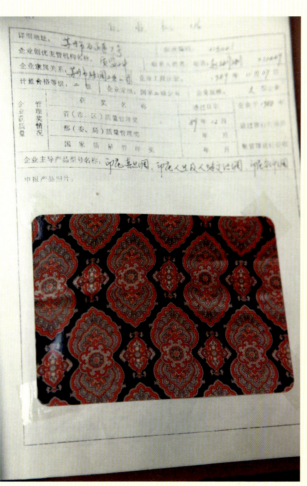

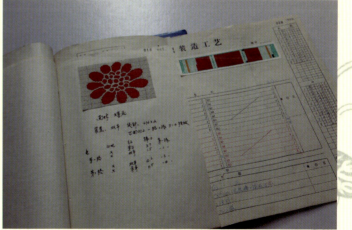

2. 纹样与意匠图
Patterns and pattern grids

纹样是丝绸面料的装饰花纹图案，意匠图是根据纹样结合织物组织将花形放大并点绘在一定格子纸（意匠纸）上的图样。丝绸织造纹样工艺中的意匠图，是近现代丝绸工业发展中所包含的一项既古老又现代的技艺档案。纹样与意匠图的设计制作，是丝绸织造工艺技术发展过程中文化、艺术等特性的完美表现。

The pattern is a decorative design on the surface of silk fabrics, while the pattern grid is a pattern which magnifies the colour pattern and dots on a gridded paper (design paper) according to the combination of the design pattern and weave structure of the fabrics. The pattern grid used in the silk weaving process is a technical archive, both ancient and modern, which is contained in the development of Suzhou silk industry in modern and contemporary times. The design and production of patterns and pattern grids perfectly reflect the characteristics of the culture and art of the silk weaving technology development.

② 匠心传承

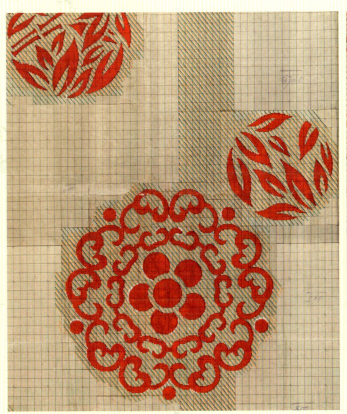

手绘设计稿 Hand-painted designs

手绘设计稿与样品说明 Hand-painted designs and sample descriptions

3. 刺绣技艺
Embroidery technology

刺绣是用针线将图案和色彩绣制在绣料（底布）上的装饰织物，距今已有两三千年的发展历史。刺绣针法为更好地传承和传播刺绣传统技艺提供了保障。花线是刺绣和机绣的主要原料，具有线条均匀、柔软光亮、色彩鲜艳丰富等特点。

Embroidery is decorative fabrics with stitched patterns, which has a history of 2,000 to 3,000 years. Embroidery stitches help inherit and spread traditional embroidery techniques better. Embroidery threads are the main materials of embroidery and machine embroidery with characteristics of evenness, softness, brightness and colourfulness.

3 古韵今声
Classical Styles in Modern Life

一、人类非物质文化遗产——苏州缂丝
Intangible Cultural Heritage of Humanity—Suzhou K'o-ssy

缂丝"龙袍" K'o-ssy dragon robe

苏州缂丝也称"刻丝",以通经断纬的方法织成,是汉族传统丝绸艺术品中的精华,素有"一寸缂丝一寸金"的盛名。苏州缂丝画与杭州丝织画、永春纸织画、四川竹帘画并称为中国"四大家织"。

Suzhou k'o-ssy which is also known as "kesi" is woven by continuous warp and broken weft yarns. Suzhou k'o-ssy is the essence of Chinese traditional silk artworks and has a reputation that "K'o-ssy has the same value as gold". Suzhou k'o-ssy painting, Hangzhou silk painting, Yongchun paper texture painting and Sichuan bamboo curtain painting are honored as "Four Home Textiles" of China.

清代缂丝"三条屏" K'o-ssy three screens from the Qing Dynasty

古韵今声

缂丝《国色天香》
K'o-ssy "National Beauty"

缂丝"宫扇"
K'o-ssy mandarin fan

缂丝"日本五条袈裟"
K'o-ssy five Japanese cassock

缂丝《拙政园观景》
K'o-ssy "Landscapes of the Humble Administrator's Garden"

二、人类非物质文化遗产——苏州宋锦
Intangible Cultural Heritage of Humanity—Suzhou Song Brocade

宋锦因发展于宋代而得名，盛于明清两代。自南宋以来，苏州宋锦、南京云锦、四川蜀锦并称全国三大名锦，有着中国"锦绣之冠"的美誉。中心馆藏的明代"米黄色地万字双鸾团龙纹宋锦"残片，再现了古代宋锦的魅力。

Song brocade is named for the development in the Song Dynasty and flourished in the Ming and Qing Dynasties. Since the Southern Song Dynasty, Suzhou Song brocade, Nanjing Yun brocade and Sichuan Shu brocade are called as "Three Famous Brocades" of China with the honor of "Brocade Champion". The fragment of "Song brocade with two phoenixes around a dragon on a beige swastika ground" from the Ming Dynasty which is collected in the administration recurs the charm of ancient Song brocade.

明代（1368—1644年）米黄色地万字双鸾团龙纹宋锦残片
Fragment of "Song brocade with two phoenixes around a dragon on a beige swastika ground" from the Ming Dynasty(1368-1644)

宋锦科技档案与样品说明
Science and technology archives of Song brocade and sample descriptions

三、国家级非物质文化遗产——苏绣
National Intangible Cultural Heritage—Suzhou Embroidery

苏绣《孔雀羽绣》
Suzhou embroidery "Embroidered Peacock"

苏绣是苏州地区刺绣产品的总称，是我国"四大名绣"之一。苏绣具有图案秀丽、构思巧妙、绣工细致、针法活泼、色彩清雅的独特风格，地方特色浓郁。

Suzhou embroidery, the general name of embroideries products from Suzhou, is one of the "Four Famous Embroideries" of China. The unique styles of Suzhou embroidery include beautiful pattern, ingenious conception, fine workmanship, lively needlework, elegant color and strong local characteristics.

苏绣《青花瓷瓶》
Suzhou embroidery "Blue-and-white Porcelain"

苏绣《朗士宁牡丹》
Suzhou embroidery "Peony"

苏绣《瓦雀栖枝》系列
A series of Suzhou embroidery "Sparrows Resting on the Branch"

四、省级非物质文化遗产——漳缎
Provincial Intangible Cultural Heritage—Zhangduan

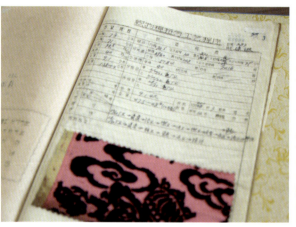

漳缎始于明末清初，因其在织物结构上创新了原有素绒织物，故成为最具艺术特色的以缎纹为地、绒经起花结构的全真丝提花绒织物。

Zhangduan dates from the late Ming and early Qing Dynasties. It innovated based on original plain velvet fabrics and becomes the most artistic product with the jacquard velvet pattern made by pure silk. It is satinweave grounded and figured by pile warp.

3 古韵今声

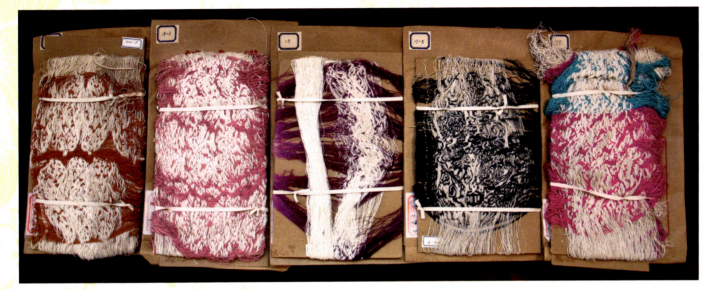

漳缎祖本：想要在目力所及范围内展示出漳缎的独特织法，就不得不借助于一些较粗的丝线，由这种粗丝线展示了具体织法的样本被称为"祖本"。

Some coarse silk yarns have to be used to illustrate the unique weaving pattern of Zhangduan in vision. The samples demonstrating the specific weaving pattern of Zhangduan is called as "The Original".

五、省级非物质文化遗产——四经绞罗
Provincial Intangible Cultural Heritage—Four-and-complex Gauze

四经绞罗是一种始自战国的织造技艺，其织物在中国古代是最好的夏季服装面料。清末民初之际，四经绞罗织造工艺曾逐渐湮没，直至20世纪八九十年代方恢复。

Four-and-complex gauze is a weaving technique derived from the Warring States. It was the best summer fabric during ancient China. The weaving technique of four-and-complex gauze was gradually lost in the late Qing Dynasty and early Republic of China and recovered in the 1980s and 1990s.

六、省级非物质文化遗产——纱罗
Provincial Intangible Cultural Heritage—Gauze

纱罗织物是由地、绞两个系统经纱与一个系统纬纱构成的经纱相互扭绞的织物。其透气性好，结构稳定，可作夏季服装、蚊帐等日用织物。

Gauze was twistingly woven by two warp systems (ground and doup warp yarns) and one weft system. Gauze is excellent at permeability and stable at structure. It can be used as fabrics of daily use such as summer garments, mosquito nets.

吴罗宫扇
Wu gauze mandarin fan

横罗
Warp ribbed gauze

折枝牡丹三经绞罗
Three-and-complex gauze with peonies

如意纹花罗
Gauze with ruyi pattern

菱形横罗
Diamond-shaped warp ribbed gauze

4 惊艳世界

Striving Surprise to the World

一、塔夫绸
Taffeta

　　塔夫绸质地轻薄平挺，织纹细密，光泽柔和，色牢度好，是高级丝绸衣料。1950年塔夫绸第一次在东欧七国展出，轰动东欧市场，此后苏州生产的塔夫绸被称为"塔王"，畅销欧美市场。1981年英国戴安娜王妃结婚礼服所选用的水榭牌深青莲色塔夫绸，就是由苏州东吴丝织厂和苏州染丝厂合作生产的。

　　Taffeta is an elegant fabric with a feature of thin and flat in texture, compact in the weave, gentle in luster, excellent in color fastness. Taffeta which was exhibited in seven countries of Eastern European for the first time in 1950 caused a sensation in the Eastern European market. Since then, the taffeta made in Suzhou was called "King Taffeta" and became popular in European and American markets. The wedding dress of Britain's Princess Diana adopted amaranth purple Taffeta with brand "Shuixie" which was manufactured by cooperation of Suzhou Dongwu Silk Weaving Factory and Suzhou Silk Dying Factory in 1981.

1981年英国皇室为戴安娜王妃婚礼购买苏州丝绸的订单与样本
The order and sample of Suzhou silk for Princess Diana's wedding by the Britain Royalty in 1981

塔夫绸科技档案
Scientific and technological archives of Taffeta

二、真丝印花绸
Printing Silk

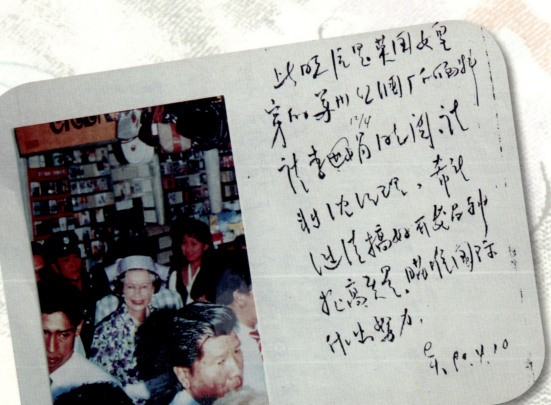

印花是用染料或颜料在织物上施印花纹的工艺过程。真丝印花绸是富有艺术性的产品，英国女王伊丽莎白二世在一次出访中，就身着苏州丝绸印花厂生产的真丝印花绸所制作的时装，使真丝印花绸风靡一时。

Printing is a process to use dyes or pigments printed on textile fabrics. Printing silk is an artistic product which was all the rage after Queen Elizabeth II dressed a costume made of printing silk made by Suzhou Silk Printing Plant during a visiting activity.

英国女王伊丽莎白二世身着真丝印花绸时装的影像资料
Image data of Queen Elizabeth II dressing a costume made of printing silk

惊艳世界

三、APEC 服装面料
APEC Fabric

该档案为2014年北京APEC会议晚宴上各经济体领导人和代表拍摄"全家福"时所穿的特色中式服装选用的面料,包括不同特质的"和美绉、天香缎、天丽绸、天娇锦"系列丝绸面料,以及具有东方韵味、耐磨性与平整度较好的宋锦。这些面料华而不炫,贵而不显,蕴含大量中国传统元素,让丝绸成为传播与弘扬中国民族传统服饰文化的载体。

This archive is the characteristic Chinese style fabrics which were used by economics leaders and representatives in APEC 2014 banquet. It includes a series of silk fabrics with different characteristics, such as Hemei crepe, Tianxiang brocaded satin, Tianli brocaded silk, Tianjiao brocade and Song brocade which is of oriental charm, excellent abrasive resistance and good evenness. These fabrics are gorgeous without dazzle, rich without flaunt, full of traditional Chinese elements, making silk be a carrier of propagation and promotion of Chinese culture of traditional costume.

宋锦 Song brocade

漳缎 Zhangduan

天香缎 Tianxiang brocaded satin

天丽绸 Tianli brocaded silk

和美绉 Hemei crepe

绢 Spun silk

锦 Brocade

绨 Bengaline

绒 Velvet

呢 Suiting silk

绡 Chiffon

纱 Gauze